# Angel of Light,
# Angel of Night

# Angel of Light,
# Angel of Night

## A True Story of Love
## and the Supernatural

**Wallace Hoffman**

Also by the same author:
*For Right and Freedom: A Marine's Rite of Passage*

To Ruth and Pam,
who both captured my heart

# Chapter 1

It was 1968—the era of the Vietnam conflict, the flowering of the hippie movement, and the revival of witchcraft.

I had just completed a four-year enlistment in the Marines after serving eighteen months in Vietnam. Upon returning to my hometown of Salt Lake City, I had rented an inexpensive apartment in the hills above the downtown area called The Avenues, a neighborhood of charming old Victorian homes intermixed with more modern residences. My place was upstairs in an old house that had been remodeled and converted into six units—three upstairs and three downstairs. My room was just big enough for a bed, a bookcase, and a comfortable chair in which I could read. In addition, I had a step-down kitchen and a shower.

I had saved three thousand dollars in the Marines, and this, along with a part-time job as a janitor, kept me going for the next eight months.

About a week after I had moved into my apartment, I met the most beautiful girl I had ever seen. I had done a small favor for my landlady, an attractive woman in her late thirties, and was eating a piece of cake which I had been given as a reward. As I sat at the kitchen table, my nerves were suddenly electrified as her daughter walked into the room. She paused in the middle of a sentence when she realized I was present, but before I had even looked up from my plate, I told myself that no woman could be so beautiful as to cause what I was feeling. It was as if high voltage electricity was surging through my body.

When I turned and looked at her, I was simply awestruck. I had sometimes contemplated how beautiful God's wife must be if he was married, and here it was as if I was standing in her presence. Her blue eyes had the serenity of the evening sky, her translucent ivory skin radiated an inner light, and her hair cascaded to her shoulders in a golden mist like a waterfall scattering drops of sunlight.

I sensed that she felt something too, and she quickly finished what she was saying and left to go on an errand to the corner store for her mother. When I left the house a short time later, she was just returning, and I resolved to say "Hi" if it was the last thing I ever did. We both greeted each other at the same time, and I had the distinct impression that she had wanted to say something as much as I had.

I learned later that her name was Ruth—straight from the Bible—and that although she appeared to be sixteen or eighteen, in reality she was only thirteen. And I was twenty-five! I told myself to forget her, knowing in the same instant that I never could. I knew inside that Ruth was the girl I was destined to marry. I would just have to wait until she was eighteen and keep my feelings to myself. I felt like the Biblical Jacob waiting for Rachel.

When I met my landlord, a sophisticated looking man in his early fifties who was somewhat overweight, I noticed that his left arm was missing. I learned later that Frank had been a former soldier in the German army during World War II and had lost his arm as a result of being wounded and captured by the Russians. After being dragged to Russia in chains in the dead of winter, he had been placed in a primitive room where a doctor had simply pointed to each man who had been wounded and ordered "amputee, amputee, amputee," without even examining the men's wounds. Although Frank's wound had been only superficial, he had been strapped to a crude wooden table and, amidst the screams in a room full of prisoners suffering a similar fate, the lower part of his arm had been cut off with a common handsaw. No anesthetic had been used. Because gangrene had set in, the operation had had to be repeated. Then because gangrene had set in again, the arm had to be amputated a third time, this time at the shoulder. Another prisoner went around the room gathering up the severed limbs in a bucket.

After getting married, Frank slept in a separate room from his wife because he would often wake up screaming at night and his bed would be soaked with perspiration as if someone had poured buckets of water on it.

However, despite his misfortune, my landlord could do the work of several men. I often did odd jobs with him remodeling the old homes he had purchased and converted to apartments. He would pick up a nail, jam it into the wall with his bare fist, and then drive it in the rest of the way with a hammer. The apartments and his real estate business provided for his family.

One day I helped Frank re-roof the apartment house in which I lived. He stood on top of the roof holding a rope, which was tied around my waist, while I laid down the asphalt shingles. After we had climbed down the ladder, a little girl in the neighborhood stared at him aghast and exclaimed, "Where's your other arm?" Frank simply replied offhandedly, "Oh, I left it home today because I didn't need it."

Whenever I went over to Frank's house to work with him, he would greet me by saying, "How are you today, Wally?" Without thinking, I would reply, "Oh, pretty good." Frank would then say, "Pretty and good, huh? Well, that's nice." It always exasperated me that he would catch me off guard.

Because I would not accept any pay for my help, I was occasionally invited for dinner. During this precious time, I sometimes had the opportunity to look at Ruth when she made a remark, without arousing suspicion. At other times I went with her family for cool walks in the evening near a second home they owned at Summit Park in the mountains. Sometimes I found myself alone with Ruth while her parents strolled on ahead. I never felt the difference in our ages. I had always looked much younger than my years, and as her father had told me, Ruth had always acted like a mature woman even as a child, possessing the natural poise and gracefulness of a princess. Ruth always gave me a special feeling when I was with her, as if I was truly myself only when I was in her presence, and as if the earth had been transformed into a paradise.

Frank's three-story house in Summit Park, the construction of which was almost finished, amazed me. He had built the place with the help of his wife and her brother Nephi. It was a gorgeous home, except for one thing. The walls were all crooked! They were out as much as an inch from top to bottom. When I pointed this out to Frank, he insisted that everything was fine and that nobody would notice it. However, I later regretted that I had ever mentioned it, for the next time I visited their home, the walls had all been straightened! Frank and Nephi had performed the excruciating job of pulling all the nails in the joists which secured the walls to the upper floors throughout the house and then re-nailing them after the walls had been straightened. Having worked as a carpenter on construction for a year before joining the Marines, I knew this would have been pure hell, as the upper floors of Frank's house had already been installed, and as a result the nails would have been almost impossible to remove.

At home in my apartment, I sometimes pondered my future. Could it ever really be possible that Ruth would be mine? It seemed too wonderful to be true. And yet how could I bear to live without her?

Then a series of strange events began to occur.

# Chapter 2

Several months had gone by since my money had run out, and I was now working in a cabinet shop. I had procured the job by offering to work the first week free, with no obligation to hire me on their part if my work proved unsatisfactory. I was put on the payroll after only two days.

It had now been about a year since I had first met Ruth. One night I was suddenly awakened by footsteps falling on the stairs leading to my apartment. It was easy to know whenever anybody came up the stairs because they creaked and groaned as if they had not been properly nailed together. However, these footsteps seemed to shake the whole house, and I thought that whoever it was, he must be huge. Suddenly, a black form entered my room, walked directly to my bed, and raised his arm holding what I thought must be a lead pipe. I did not have time to be afraid. My first reaction was simple astonishment, since I knew I had locked the door. I tensed as the arm descended, knowing that in the next instant, I would be dead. However, the impact of the blow seemed to disperse the form itself, and I found myself alone in the darkness, my nerves numb from apprehension. I climbed out of bed and checked the door. The door was still locked.

Since I could not explain the incident, I simply dismissed it. Then several weeks later, I was again suddenly awakened by heavy footsteps on the stairs. *What is this, a repeat performance?* I thought sarcastically. I was not going to be scared by some phantom. However, this time the footsteps passed my door and walked around the corner to the next apartment. I heard someone knocking at the door. I knew a young woman, whom I'll call Lynn, lived there. We had never become acquainted, but occasionally I had said hello in passing. Suddenly, I heard the door open, then a gasp as from the sudden intake of air, and then the most harrowing scream I had ever heard. The scream went on and on, as if someone was falling into a bottomless pit and was confronting new horrors each instant, only to be finally engulfed by a fathomless abyss of darkness and despair beyond imagination.

I can never forget that scream. It was not produced by any earthly terror. It was far beyond that. At first, I was too stunned to move. Then my reason asserted itself. *She must have been attacked*, I heard myself thinking. *Get moving!* Another part of me argued, *No way!* Then again—*You're an ex-Marine. Now get moving, you coward, or you'll never be able to live with yourself.*

I jumped out of bed, fumbled for my trousers, but then decided there was no time to get dressed. I flung open the door. It was only several steps to Lynn's apartment. But her door was closed. I hadn't heard the door close! *Perhaps her assailant was just on the other side with a knife or a gun*, I thought. *Better break down the door. No, what would happen if I break into some woman's place in the middle of the night wearing only my shorts!*

I called out Lynn's name. No answer. I stood back to kick down the door. However, just as I braced myself for the effort, I heard a voice say, "It's okay...I'm okay...I just had a nightmare."

The next day I happened to meet Lynn on the sidewalk as I was leaving and asked her what had happened. She said, "You know, it's funny. I don't remember a thing. All I remember is you calling my name."

Once again, I tried to dismiss the incident. But I had heard the footsteps, the knock at the door, and the door opening *before* I had heard the scream. It just did not make sense.

Over the years, I have asked myself if it was possible that all of this could have occurred in my own mind. I don't mean if I could have imagined it, because we all know the difference between what we imagine and real life. But was it possible for the mind to experience something that was as real—no, more real—than life itself, yet which never really happened in physical reality but only in the mind? Or was it possible for consciousness to perceive events in a reality that was not this one, but just as real? I knew one thing—my mind could never have imagined that scream. Even my words are inadequate to describe it. It filled my soul with sheer terror.

# Chapter 3

One night after work I was unlocking the door to my apartment when Lynn suddenly appeared with an attractive young woman whom she introduced as her cousin Pam, telling her that I was the brave young man who had come to her rescue. They asked me if I would like to join them later in the evening with Don, a college student who lived in the apartment next door, and enjoy some popcorn while we watched TV. I hesitated for a moment—I usually studied at night—

but then decided I needed a change and accepted.

The evening went quickly. Lynn, Pam, and Don seemed to enjoy themselves, laughing and talking, but I was silent most of the time. However, no one seemed to mind, and Pam even seemed to like me that way. When I left, Lynn told me she would be gone for a few days and asked me if I would watch out for Pam. "Just be there in case anything happens," she said. I promised her I would.

The next night, after showering and shaving, I knocked on Lynn's door and asked Pam if she would like to come over to get better acquainted. I thought she would refuse, but I figured I had nothing to lose but my pride. She hesitated for a moment, but then seemed to realize that there was nothing better to do and accepted. Or perhaps she concluded that I would probably not have the nerve to ask her again.

We began by discussing literature— books we had both read—somewhat awkwardly at first, but both of us relaxing more as the evening wore on. I was surprised I had not noticed Pam's beauty the night before. I had thought she was somewhat attractive, but now I could see she was really beautiful. However, it was a cold beauty, not a radiant one like Ruth's.

The next evening my hair was just drying from the shower when I heard a knock at the door. When I opened it, Pam was standing on the threshold in a stunning dress which ended several inches above her knees. She had beautiful legs. I felt my face flush, but Pam simply smiled at the compliment and walked inside.

That night I kissed Pam for the first time. But having no previous experience, I did not know how to go about it and stopped from embarrassment. I was surprised that I had felt nothing, but Pam did not seem to mind.

I do not remember what we talked about, but during a pause in one conversation Pam suddenly looked up from where she was sitting on the floor and asked, "What would you do if I was the devil?"

I suddenly felt uneasy, but then I told myself she was only nineteen, and it was not uncommon for young people to feel alienated or think at times that they might be crazy or whatever. "You couldn't be," I replied, as if to reassure her. "The devil, if he exists, is a spirit." She did not reply, but seemed to be having thoughts of her own. I thought it strange that she should ask such a question, for it was not related to anything we were discussing.

Later, I told Pam that I had to get some sleep. This was the third night I had been up late, and my job at the cabinet shop was demanding. I was exhausted. When she asked if she could stay with me the rest of the night, I simply assented with nothing in mind except to get a good night's sleep.

As we lay in bed, Pam asked me to run my fingers through her hair. A moment later, I was unbuttoning her dress, not because I was physically aroused, but simply to feel the form and intimacy of her body.

I must have fallen asleep, because the next instant I was literally jolted awake as if by high-voltage electricity. I found myself lying on my back, Pam was laying on her side staring at me in the darkness, and *I had the distinct impression that she was trying to possess my body!* My blood felt like ice, but I concealed my feelings. *This is insane!* I thought.

After a moment she asked, "Do you feel better?" I had no idea if I had been asleep ten minutes or several hours. As we lay in bed, Pam suddenly brought her leg across my body. I felt myself becoming aroused, not out of any inner desire, but out of the sheer physical stimulation of her body against mine. I suddenly realized she wanted to make love. In the same instant I realized that giving herself to a man is the greatest gift a woman can offer, and that for a man to refuse is the greatest insult. I thought of Ruth. I knew I loved her more than Pam. But there was no guarantee she would marry me. Perhaps it was only my own fantasy. And she was so much younger than me. I decided at that moment to marry Pam.

It might seem strange that I could make such an abrupt decision. But although I had only known Pam a few days, there was a natural rapport between us, as if we had always known each other. It was never as if we were strangers, but friends who had not immediately recognized each other. My love for her might have been incomplete, but it was in no way superficial, and her smile always touched my heart.

When we came together, it was suddenly as if we were both suspended in the cold darkness of space. But more— whereas before we had been two separate beings, I was now astonished to find we had literally become one. I was not simply inside her body, *but inside her very soul*. I found myself wondering—if *sex is the mystical union of two human beings, then how can others not know that the spiritual dimension is real?*

I suddenly began to dread that I might never complete the act. I began to realize that sex cannot be motivated simply by the desire to please your partner. Unless you also sought your own selfish pleasure, you might fail miserably. But then I thought—*if sex is a selfish act, how can it be a spiritual experience?*

If it had not been for the sudden contractions within her body, I could never have reached climax. But the contractions did not seem like the spontaneous release of an all-consuming passion. Was it possible for a woman to fake it?

We were both drenched in sweat. The total lack of stimulation made me feel as if I had intentionally profaned this most sacred of all acts, as if I had engaged in a ritual not of uncontrolled desire, but one of cold, calculated purpose—as if I was totally responsible for what I had done.

As I lay on my back thinking that this was the hardest work I had ever performed, Pam said, "You didn't enjoy it, did you?" I said nothing. Then she said, "Don't you know you are supposed to close your eyes?" This startled me, for I suddenly realized that she had been watching me in the darkness, and I had not been aware of anything but my own thoughts.

In the morning, I showered and got ready for work while Pam slept. Then I sat in a chair and contemplated the innocent face of the young woman who slept in my bed. I knew this had not been her first time. She had had several other boyfriends. I also knew she took birth control pills. After a moment, she opened her eyes and smiled. Then she climbed out of bed and stood before me fully naked while she stretched. I looked at her supple, delicate body and was surprised that the only feeling it aroused in me was a quiet admiration for the female form and a sense of wonder.

"Don't you know that what we did last night was wrong?" she asked.

"Anyone who would say that has a warped mind," I replied.

Pam walked with me the two blocks it took to get to the bus stop where I caught a ride to work weekdays. When the bus pulled up and opened its doors, I took Pam into my arms and kissed her. I knew that this was what she wanted—to have people gaping and gawking at us out the windows. She smiled radiantly as I looked at the laughter in her eyes. I boarded the bus, but as it drove off I realized only too late that I should have waved to her out the window. When I looked back, I could see her walking away dejectedly, her disappointment in every step. I cursed myself. I was such a klutz.

# Chapter 4

The next day was Saturday, and we ran barefoot through the park in the pouring rain and played on the swings. Somehow Pam knew I wanted to do this at least once in my life, just like in the movies. Later, she exchanged her wet clothes for some of my dry ones. My blue shirt and white shorts made her look like the tomboy she had been as a child. And strangely, it made her look even more feminine.

When it stopped raining, we went back outside. Upon returning, I discovered the key to my apartment was missing. I did not know where I might have lost it, so we walked the block to my landlord's house and I rang the bell. When Frank answered the door, I explained that I had lost my key, but as I did so, Ruth came to the door to see who it was. However, she left immediately when she saw Pam wearing my clothes.

Later, Pam asked me, "What would you do if I got pregnant?"

"I would marry you," I replied. "I want to anyway," I said. "Would you marry me?"

This caught her off guard. I suddenly realized she did not love me at all. Or rather, she loved me only for the moment. It was like she had told me before—nothing is permanent. You only kill what you try to preserve. Each moment must be lived and enjoyed for itself as the unique experience it is.

"Why should I marry you when I can marry someone who I like just as much, but who has money?" she replied.

I admired her for her honesty. That was the way it was between us. We did not try to fake it. Reality was and is what it is. We accepted both the beauty and the tragedy of life—like children.

"If I married you, I wouldn't cook your meals, wash your dishes, or do your laundry," she said.

However, she did do the dishes for me just once, because she knew that without asking, I wanted her to. And she smiled when I put my arms around her waist and kissed her on the cheek.

Another time she told me, as if making an accusation, that I did not need anyone. In some ways, this was true. At home while I was growing up, I had often fixed my meals, did the dishes, and cleaned the house. "I'm not your slave," my mother had told me. I learned to take care of myself.

I did not know that a woman would not stay with a man if she did not feel needed.

Sometimes we had stormy arguments, but just when I thought everything was lost,

Pam would kneel upon the floor beside me, slip her arms around my legs, and rest her head against my knees. Sometimes I was hard on her, seeing how far I could go as a test of her feeling for me. At other times, I expressed feelings that I should have kept secret, but which had been buried too long. It was depressing. After one such confession, Pam took my tennis racket to the grade school down the street and began batting the ball despondently against the wall. When I came for her a few moments later, she was fluttering all over the pavement chasing the ball, utterly captivating, like a beautiful butterfly.

However, she made demands on me too. Unlike Ruth, who seemed to fuel me with energy, Pam continually drained my resources by her constant need for attention. I realized that she could never be alone. She could not occupy herself for long. She always had to be doing something with someone.

It was near the Fourth of July, and I had bought some "glow worms," or small disc-shaped tablets that magically grow like worms when lit on fire. It had been a long time since I had played with them as a boy. Pam and I were sitting on the sidewalk with Don in front of the house when Pam said, "What pattern shall we arrange them in? Oh, I know. Let's arrange them in the form of a cross!" She quickly did so and lit them on fire. As I watched the "worms" eerily grow out of the burning cross amidst dense black clouds of smoke, I had the uneasy feeling that I had somehow profaned the crucifixion of Christ. The cross etched itself into the pavement, leaving a black mark, as if the place where I lived had now been cursed. Several weeks later, I removed it with a hammer and chisel.

# Chapter 5

It was Sunday, and I had now known Pam for five days. There was not much to do, and we were both bored. Pam was lying on my bed with her head propped up on one arm looking at me as I sat on the floor at her feet. I was in a sarcastic mood. Pam had taught me something which I had not known before. There are some women who envy the strength and power of a man and who like being women only when they discover the greater power which they possess over a man as the result of their beauty. A man is like a powerful machine which they can drive and control with the slightest touch of their foot on the accelerator or the turn of the steering wheel. Was this the reason I could not fully respond to her?

I stared straight into Pam's eyes with a derisive smile on my face. I expected her to look away from the intensity of my gaze, but her eyes simply remained on mine, her face expressionless. I knew she was using her defenselessness as a weapon. I continued to look directly into her eyes, daring her to look away first. I was purposely being obnoxious. I soundlessly challenged her to read my thoughts. *You don't have any power over me,* I said in my mind. She still didn't look away, so I pushed her harder. *Read my mind! You don't have any power over me. You can't control my life. I'm free, and I'll live my life as I choose!*

Suddenly, her eyes literally changed into those of a demon and emitted beams of energy which were so powerful that they hit me with the full force of a freight train. It was as if space itself had shattered. At the moment of impact I was astonished to discover that my will power had totally vanished. It was as if I felt the crushing blow with my spirit while my body remained completely motionless. I thought, *My God, I have no control over my body!* My mind was perfectly clear, but I had absolutely no power whatever to move a muscle. It was not as if I was pinned down. There was simply no connection between my will and my body.

While to all outside appearances, I might have appeared normal, this force was literally crushing me within myself. I suddenly realized that this force was more powerful than any known to man, greater even than electricity or atomic energy. I knew that there was no way I could withstand it. Then in the next instant I thought, *Oh my God, I'm dead.*

I imagined my body being discovered with no clue as to the cause of death—probably diagnosed as a heart attack—and no one ever knowing what had really happened.

At that moment, Pam looked away saying, "Don't do that!" In the same instant, I was released from the inconceivable power which held me in its control.

I can never forget the incredible contempt and fury of those demonic eyes whose pride and power I had challenged. It was as if they were screaming, *"You miserable mortal, you're less than the dust of the earth. This isn't even the beginning of what I could do!"*

We never discussed this experience. Somehow, I could not bring it up, and Pam seemed to avoid it. I knew something in my expression or my eyes had made Pam uneasy or filled her with fear and that perhaps she was unaware of the power that had emanated from her being. Could it be she was possessed with an evil spirit without knowing it? With her interest in the powers of the occult—I knew she had played with an Ouija board—had she opened herself up to the unknown forces of darkness?

That night my mother stopped by on her way back from California. My parents were living in Kansas and my mother needed a place to stay for the night. I resented her intrusion. She never asked me in advance if she could stay with me. Because she was my mother, she felt she never needed to ask anything. We had never had a good relationship.

Pam was still wearing my clothes, so when my mother saw her, she immediately knew the situation. Mom was furious that I had a girlfriend. I had always been shy, and in high school, she had pushed me to go to dances as a way of mocking me. The room seemed to fill with black clouds from her fury, not that I could see them, but I could certainly feel them. Pam excused herself and went back to Lynn's apartment.

I told my mother that I would get her a room in a motel, but that she could not stay with me that night. The Biblical scripture kept going through my mind—*Therefore shall a man leave his father and his mother, and shall cleave unto his wife: and they shall be one flesh* (Genesis 2:24). I felt that I had to make a choice, and I had made it.

My mother was furious that I should prefer anyone other than her. It seemed she could not stand that I spend another minute with this girl. She said that she could move the top mattress of my bed onto the floor and sleep on that, and began moving towards the bed, but I blocked her access. I told her my decision was final and stressed again I would get her a motel room, but that she could not stay with me that night.

She refused the motel room and left in tears and rage. I knew she was trying to make me feel guilty, as if I had turned her out into the night with no place to go. Instilling guilt was her method, and she had succeeded. I did feel guilty and ashamed. It was only years later that I learned she had phoned her friend from the gas station across the street and stayed with her that night. I could imagine everything she had told her.

After my mother had left, I went over to Lynn's apartment and knocked on the door. Pam opened it wearing a filmy orange see-through nightgown. She radiated happiness that I had chosen her over my mother, but I felt miserable and depressed. As we sat on the floor and talked, Pam suddenly interrupted me and asked me to make love to her.

Now it is the nature of the human mind that we cannot always control the thoughts that enter our brain, and sometimes those thoughts even shock us because they are so inappropriate to the situation at hand or to our character. Thus I smiled slightly when I recalled an extremely obscene remark my landlord had made. And because Pam could easily read my face, she insisted that I tell her what I was thinking. I refused, but Pam kept on insisting. So I finally relented, since it was part of our intimate relationship to keep nothing from each other. However, I immediately regretted it, as Pam got up, turned on the TV, and began watching a horror movie. She loved horror movies.

I slept alone that night.

# Chapter 6

The next day Lynn was due to arrive home, and Pam would return to Idaho where she lived with her parents.

In the morning, Pam walked me to the bus stop. Only six days ago I had met her for the first time. This time I did not take her in my arms and kiss her. I simply gazed into her eyes as she smiled, and then I said goodbye.

As the bus pulled off, I waved to her out the window, and she waved back gaily. However, I did not prolong our farewell until she had vanished from sight. I purposely turned and faced the front of the bus until the last possible moment, and then I turned around to watch her walking away. I could tell by the bounce in her step that this was the way she had wanted it to be.

When I returned home that night, there was a note under my door with Pam's name and address on it. I tore it up and threw it away. I would not chase after her as her other boyfriends had done.

In the weeks that followed, Pam was constantly on my mind, and the torment of her absence was like the pain of being stabbed with a thousand knives whenever I thought of her. I regretted destroying her note. I could not bring myself to ask Lynn for Pam's address.

Don told me later that he had not hit it off with Pam. She had asked him what he thought about the hippies, and he had given the wrong answer—"a bunch of misguided kids who are wasting their lives." She had asked me the same question. I had told her that what they had started was beautiful— the flowers, the bright colors, the search for genuine values—until it had become commercialized. We were thinking on the same frequency.

A few months later, I was going through an old used bookstore looking for something on the occult. I hoped to understand more fully what I had just been through. Had Pam been involved in witchcraft or Satanism? Was she unknowingly possessed of the devil, or had she sold her soul in return for her powers? Did the abortion she had had earlier in her life after she had been raped have anything to do with it? Why was I not afraid of her? Was it because I knew that evil could have no power over me unless I gave my consent? But then—had I imperiled my own soul by making love to her?

As I looked through the books, I suddenly had the distinct premonition that the young girl at the front desk was a witch. She had red hair and a good figure—one I realized other men would find attractive— but there was a hardness to her beauty that left me cold. Without thinking further, I approached her and blurted out, "Pardon me, miss, but are you a witch?"

I had no sooner asked the question than I felt like a fool. But she simply replied straightforwardly, "No, I'm not now, but I used to be."

I was about to laugh and apologize, but I suddenly realized she was telling the truth. Something in the way I had asked her made her realize that I was sincere.

"I knew a woman who possessed supernatural powers," I told her, "and I would greatly appreciate any information you could give me."

"I know a book on the subject," she replied, "but I don't have time right now to look for it. I'm just leaving on my lunch break, and I'm meeting a girl at a bar."

Like a blockhead, I followed her out the door, asking her questions as we walked. I was astonished to discover that although she had practiced what she called "white witchcraft," she did not believe in the devil. She simply believed that there were powers of darkness which could be used for either good or evil depending upon how they were controlled, and that witchcraft was the science of learning how to use them properly to achieve beneficial results. Such powers were not evil in themselves, as many people supposed.

At the bar, she ignored me while she ate lunch with her friend. I sat foolishly drinking a coke, until I realized she thought I was trying to pick her up. Then I interrupted her long enough to thank her for the information she had given me and walked away. However, as I left, she suddenly became aware that my motives were genuine. "Wait a minute," she called as she ran up to me. "There's a book called *The Black Arts* which might help you." I thanked her kindly and left.

Years later, I found a copy of the book, but somehow I could never bring myself to read it.

Lynn later tried to commit suicide. I never found out why. I learned from Don that she was in the hospital. She had always seemed like an emotionally unstable person.

Had she also been involved in a cult?  Was I part of some diabolical scheme that she and Pam had devised?  And if so, had it failed or succeeded?

Was I becoming paranoid?

The cabinet shop for which I worked closed down due to financial problems after I had worked there a year.  I got a job at the Holy Cross Hospital a few blocks away working in the stockroom.

# Chapter 7

I continued to help Frank out occasionally. I painted the outside of the apartment house in which I lived with two coats of paint. I always kept the yard free of weeds and the lawn mowed. I even laid a brick patio out back to save Frank the effort and installed tile in the shower of my apartment—which had simply been painted before—and took sponge baths at night until the work was completed. I was still invited to dinner.

If Frank ever needed a tool while he worked, which he did not have, he would set everything aside, put on a suit, and go to the hardware store and buy it. Why he would take the time to put on a suit mystified me until years later I realized it was because of his immense German pride. He had told me that when you were dressed in a suit, the sales clerks were friendly and treated you well, whereas if you were not, sometimes they were inconsiderate and rude. I also realized that this was the same reason he sold real estate and bought old houses to remodel and convert to apartments. He could never stand to have anyone tell him what to do, as would be the case in a regular job. If, when we were working, I made a suggestion which he knew was right, he would say, "Okay, you're the boss. You're the man with the brass nuts." I knew it was his way of saving face.

One day as we were working, I asked Frank, "What do you think God had in mind when he created woman?" Frank replied, "Oh, God didn't create woman. What really happened was that God started to create woman, but about half way through he had to go to the bathroom. While he was gone, Satan crept in and finished the job. When God returned, he was shocked to see what had happened. But then on second thought, he said, "Hmm…not bad, not bad at all."

Another day Frank's wife did something during lunch which upset him. For a full five minutes, Frank ranted and raved at the top of his lungs. Frank was a large man, and the volume of his voice was like a windstorm. However, I knew this must have been a common occurrence, since Ruth and her younger sister and brother continued eating as if nothing was happening. Even his wife seemed unperturbed. For myself, it took my full concentration just to keep my legs from trembling and my fork from banging against my plate.

Occasionally Frank would pass gas while sitting at the table. With a look of shock he would say to one of his girls, "You should be ashamed of yourself, a nice girl like you letting a big fart like that." This would, of course, be followed by loud denials. At other times he might accuse his wife, which would be followed by some merriment on the part of the children.

One time I caught Frank with his pants down. It was in church, and I happened to walk past the open door of a Sunday school class, which was filled with children. Frank was sitting on a raised platform at the front of the class with several other adults, and I had never seen him so happy and delighted. He seemed like a big child himself, his head bobbing up and down as he sang the song with the children and slapping his hand against his knee in time with the music. His face immediately changed when he saw me standing in the doorway, and he quickly tried to regain his composure but it was too late. I was gone. I did not want to spoil his fun, and besides, his secret was safe with me.

I knew that Frank never wanted me to marry his daughter and would probably do everything he could to prevent it. He had told me that I was too complicated. I always thought about and analyzed everything. For me, everything was either black or white. His attitude was, why not just live life and be happy? He didn't care so much about right and wrong as not rocking the boat. Just go along with everyone else was his advice. He wanted a husband who would just make his daughter happy and who had a good job. I knew he was right. I wasn't qualified.

One evening my stockroom manager at the hospital gave me a ride home from work even though it was just a few blocks to my apartment. It was still light and we were sitting in his car in front of my place talking when Ruth walked across the street. "That's the girl I told you about," I said. I had told him more than once about the most beautiful girl in the world. He looked at her, then looked at me and said, "I don't even think she's good looking."

He was not being rude. I knew he was simply expressing his opinion. But it was the first time that it occurred to me that someone else might not share my evaluation of her. Even Ruth herself did not think she was beautiful, and this puzzled me.

Another time I was sitting in church with Ruth's family while she gave a talk from the pulpit. It is common practice in a Mormon church to assign its members to speak. I looked at her and then at the congregation and marveled that no one but me seemed to see that here was an angel of light that had appeared to them. Then I noticed one young boy who must have had the gift of sight, as he seemed to be as enamored of her as I was. It was wonderful to have several minutes to simply gaze at Ruth's face without interruption.

Ruth's father never liked his children to take church sermons too seriously. While Ruth would be sitting with her legs crossed, Frank would dislodge her shoe with his foot or do something else to distract her. Or he might say something funny in his dry offhand manner to change the mood of the situation, such as that the speaker looked constipated or like he needed to go to the bathroom.

Lynn had moved away. However, as luck would have it, I happened to meet her again one day when she was filling her car with gas at the service station across the street. She told me that Pam had returned to Idaho and was getting married. I concealed my feelings of disappointment and said I hoped she would be happy.

I had worked at Holy Cross Hospital for a year and eight months when my parents stopped by for a visit. They wanted me to come back to Kansas and live with them while I went to college. I was now twenty-eight years old. I knew that without a college degree, I could never support Ruth. If there was even a slight chance I might have her, I had to take it. On the other hand, I didn't want to leave her, and I didn't want to become dependent upon my parents. I couldn't make up my mind. I thought that I might have to make the wrong decision before I could determine what the right decision would be. I decided to go back with my parents and see what would happen.

# Chapter 8

Lawrence, Kansas was a small, picturesque town with a quaint, distinguished university. Unlike most of Kansas, which was flat and dry, Lawrence was green with rolling hills.

My parents had a small house in a suburban neighborhood. My room was downstairs in the basement just below the kitchen. The only other resident was my younger sister who was going to college. My other three sisters and two brothers were on their own.

Everything went well the first few weeks I was there. However, I soon realized that my parents did not have the money to send both my sister and me to school. I would have to leave. However, I did not know what I would do for a living. I procrastinated and spent my days reading.

Years earlier, even before I had met Pam, I had told my mother that Ruth was the woman I wanted to marry. I was surprised that before I had even told my mother anything about her, she had insisted that Ruth was not the girl for me.

When I was in high school, my mother had planned a surprise birthday party for me. I had few friends, because I liked to be alone, and I did not even know most of the young people she had invited. About half the people left early, but the rest stayed and played games. I was trying to help others feel comfortable and enjoy the party, and I was just beginning to enjoy it myself when suddenly my mother approached me and said maliciously, "Are you having a good time?" This immediately destroyed the mood I was in, and I was glad when the party was over and everyone had left. I never understood this incident until years later, when one day it suddenly dawned on me that she had planned the party not so I would have a good time, but so I would be embarrassed and humiliated. Something clicked in my mind, as if a piece of a puzzle had fallen into place.

When my oldest sister got married to a man who had a talent for charming women, my mother told me he was the son she should have had instead of me. However, although he could take a woman's breath away, he lacked the character I could respect. Years later he had an affair with another woman and my sister divorced him.

After moving home, my mother kept asking if my savings had run out, until I had no money left. Then she began to make my life hell. She had always been a master at making sarcastic remarks or knowing how to intimidate me. Now it seemed she had an entire planned program all laid out.

I had not felt good about myself since I had moved home. I did not like being dependent upon my parents again, and since now I was not going to college, I felt I was somehow stealing from them by relying on their support. It did not feel right, and my conscience bothered me until it seemed like it was on fire.

One day I left my room to go upstairs and happened to meet my mother at the bottom of the stairs. *"How can you stand to live with yourself!"* she viciously hissed. The words stopped me cold, because it was not my mother's voice which was speaking, but Satan's. I knew that no one in the family could have known about the inner struggle I was having unless they could have read my mind. I decided then and there I would leave. I did not care what it would take.

I found a job painting a house to get enough money for bus fare, and my father drove me to the station. As I boarded the bus, I looked back at my father and said, "Goodbye, dad." But my father did not answer. He simply stood looking forlornly at me, as if from the other end of a long dark tunnel, and I felt I had somehow abandoned or deserted him. I turned so he would not see the tears in my eyes. I felt as if my heart had broken in two.

I knew now that my mother had wanted vengeance ever since I had refused to let her stay with me the last night I had been with Pam. She had wanted to have the last word. I did not care. If somehow it made up for the distress I had caused her, then so be it. Now we were even.

# Chapter 9

I stopped for a short time in Salt Lake City, but because I could not find any work, I caught a ride to California with my uncle who was visiting from Los Altos. He was part owner in a new golf course that had been built south of San Jose, and for the next three months, I spent my days digging weeds out of sand traps with a Mexican laborer while living in a dumpy apartment in San Jose. Then I worked for nine months as a carpenter building homes. Finally, I found a job working in the electronics industry testing circuit boards. I would work in electronics for the next twenty-eight years, eventually becoming an electronic engineering technician.

While still working as a carpenter, I finally found a more suitable place in Santa Clara in an old Victorian house that had been converted into five apartments. My method was to find a cheap apartment and then fix it up so that I had a decent place to live. The woodwork in my apartment had so much ornamentation that it took me three weeks to paint the place. Then it took another five weeks to dig all the weeds out of the yard. After that I mowed the lawn once a week. I never charged my landlord for my labor. I even raised my own rent occasionally so that my landlord could keep up with inflation, just as I had when I lived in The Avenues in Salt Lake City. Whenever I moved from an apartment, I always left it in the same or better condition than I had found it.

There was a woman in the neighborhood who I initially thought must be mentally disabled, but whom I later concluded must be possessed of an evil spirit. She wore black clothes and had a dumpy looking appearance. She always walked very slowly down the sidewalk, looking at the ground and her eyes darting warily from side to side as if she expected to be attacked at any moment by some unknown danger. Suddenly, for no apparent reason, she would fling her arms out to her sides as if she had been assaulted and scream a long series of incomprehensible words, which sounded strangely like profanity. Just as suddenly, she would return to her former demeanor and continue her walk. At other times, any unexpected movement or sound might set her off.

One day I looked out my front window and saw a young man approaching her on the sidewalk. I watched with anticipation, knowing that he was unaware of the approaching peril. I knew she did not see him coming, and he startled her just as he walked by. She jumped and threw out her arms, spewing forth a litany of curses. He looked back puzzled, wondering what he had done to offend her.

Another time the kids in the house next door made fun of her as she walked up the sidewalk, calling her names and screaming insults. They lived in an old run-down dilapidated house that had never been painted, there were weeds in the yard instead of a lawn, and there were empty trash cans lining the curb. Suddenly, she crossed the street and in a fury tore into the trash cans, belting them right and left. This only increased the hilarity of the children, and she walked off cursing.

I felt guilty for laughing. I never made fun of the mentally disabled or the handicapped even as a child. However, the loud banging and clattering of the trash cans was just too much.

My studio apartment had a porch that had been converted into a bedroom by nailing some slats between the pillars. You could even see light through the slats. In the summer, the spiders crawled through, and in the rainy season the cold air came through. It was hard to keep the place heated.

One day, I was lying in bed slowly drifting off to sleep. I could hear the curses of the mentally disabled lady as she walked up the street. I was in that strange twilight zone between sleep and wakefulness. Suddenly, I realized that it was not a woman who was screaming the curses, but a man. She was possessed by a male spirit! Then with astonishment I realized that I recognized the voice of the spirit who possessed her, perhaps from a pre-existent life. *"I know who that is..."* I thought, *"that's..."* But just as his name was entering my consciousness, a hand suddenly grabbed me by the back of the neck and forced my face into my pillow. Thinking that someone had entered my room and was trying to smother me, I brought my arm around forcefully to repel the intruder. But there was no one there. I got up and checked the door, but it was still bolted from the inside. There was no way anyone could have entered the room. I knew the hand I had felt had not been my imagination, nor had it been a dream. It was a real hand!

This experience made me realize that spirits can not only read our thoughts, but that we can actually feel them if they choose to make us do so, just as if they were flesh and bone.

I lived in my apartment in Santa Clara for three years. All during that time, there were two little dogs that lived in the yard of the run-down house next door. Every night they barked for two straight hours with no intermission. I complained to the owner, a large heavy man who looked in worse shape than his home, but it did no good. Finally, I got a new apartment several miles north in Sunnyvale. I would move the next day.

That night the dogs began barking about two o'clock as usual. By four o'clock, I decided that if I was going to get any sleep at all, I would have to drive up to my new apartment. I threw some bedding in my car and left.

When I arrived at my apartment, I checked the bedroom, bathroom, and closet to make sure the place was empty, and then threw some blankets on the living room floor. As I lay on my back, I thought that I could finally get a few hours sleep. I knew the door was locked and there was nothing to worry about. Strangely, all my life I had felt that I could never let my guard down or something might happen. It was a feeling of subliminal apprehension that I always carried with me. However, tonight I knew I was safe. I thought that for once in my life I could just relax. Like Dagny Taggart in the novel *Atlas Shrugged*, I thought, "*This is it. Drop the controls.*"

Just as I said the words in my mind, a deafening, ear-splitting piercing sound shattered the silence. It seemed to be right next to my head, but also filled the whole room. I felt my heart stop and my blood turn to ice. For a moment I was too stunned to move. Then I got up to find the source of the sound and found that it was emanating from a device on the wall. I had never seen or heard of smoke detectors before, which had just come out on the market. I did not know how to disable the device, so I grabbed my blankets and headed out the door. When I got to my car, I was stopped by a police officer who inquired why I was out so late at night. After telling him my story, he let me go with no further questions. I guess he figured that my tale was so implausible that I must be telling the truth.

While it might have been sheer coincidence that the smoke detector went off the moment I had decided to totally relax, I personally feel that some being must have been reading my mind and knew exactly what I had been thinking. There was simply no reason for the alarm to go off. There was no smell of smoke in the room. The place was perfectly quiet. There was no vibration or movement that could have set off the alarm. And it occurred at exactly the moment that I had decided to drop my guard. It was uncanny.

My feeling of apprehension returned.

# Chapter 10

The first encounter I had with the supernatural was when I was about five years old. It was around nine o-clock at night, and my dad had sent me to bed. I shared a bedroom with my two older sisters, but they had gone somewhere with my mother.

As I entered the doorway to my room, I was suddenly transfixed by the window on the opposite wall. It was completely filled with obscene, demonic faces peering into the room and laughing and jeering at me. It was a scene straight out of hell. I had no sooner witnessed the sight then it vanished. I quickly climbed into the top bed of the bunk bed I shared with one of my sisters and pulled the blanket over my head. The room seemed filled with the presence of evil. I was terrified. After a moment I tried to call out to my father, but was astonished to find that I could not utter a word. Knowing that I could not stay in this intolerable situation, I finally mustered the courage to jump out of bed and run out of the room. When I told my father what had happened, he said that I had just had a bad dream and to go back to bed. Fortunately, my mother and sisters walked into the house that moment, and when we went to bed, the evil presence had vanished.

When I was about twelve, my mother often arranged for me to babysit the neighbor's children so I could earn my own money. I was only a few years older than the children I tended, and I dreaded taking care of the neighbor's four boys across the street who were rowdy and impossible to control. One night as I got up from the couch to chase after them, I bumped against a table and a lamp crashed to the floor, breaking off an ornamental piece from the base. Filled with dread, I put the lamp back on its table and turned it so that the missing piece would not be noticed. Later, as I left the house, I threw the broken piece as far as I could into the darkness so it would never be found.

The children must have told their parents, for the next day, my mother angrily entered my room and told me to go over to the neighbors and apologize for my bad deed. When the children's mother answered the door, she kindly told me that the lamp had been a prized gift from a friend, and that if I simply returned the broken piece, she would have the lamp repaired.

I knew it would be impossible to find the shattered fragment. However, I had no choice except to walk over to the neighbor's lawn and begin searching for it. At the end of the lawn, there was a patch of weeds, which might also be concealing it. Since I was trespassing on someone else's property,

I had only a few moments to find it. I said a quick prayer, pleading with God for help in what seemed to me a life-and-death crisis. When I had finished, I felt something hard under my shoe. When I lifted my foot, there was the broken fragment. I returned it and received a pardon for my crime.

Later in life, when I worked in electronics, there was an unmarried Vietnamese girl at work who did rework on the electronic boards. When I first met her, I sensed the presence of black clouds which seemed to surround her and emanate from her being. I had the premonition that she had been involved in prostitution in Viet Nam and may have even determined the fate of some individual's lives. One day I asked another worker what he thought of her. "She is pure evil," he said. Surprised, I asked for an explanation. "I can't tell you why," he insisted. "All I know is that she is pure evil." I later learned that she had her own home, and that it was paid off. I wondered where she had got the money.

I remember from watching TV that a woman who had been raped described her attacker as having eyes whose pupils actually burned like red hot coals from hell. She said that this was not her imagination, but that a red fire actually emanated from his pupils.

We have all seen in comics or the movies where evil beings emit powerful beams of energy from their eyes. Why would anyone even imagine that such a thing was possible unless perhaps subconsciously we know that it is? Could it be that the mind knows more than it admits?

# Chapter 11

If there is a devil, then there is a God. Otherwise, Satan would have total power.

I believe that anyone can contact the supernatural dimension and know that it is real, although it is easier to make contact with supernatural evil than good. Those who dabble in the occult may find themselves possessed of powers far beyond their control, and which may destroy their very soul.

While I have experienced the forces of evil, I have also experienced the Spirit of

God. For myself, I found this difficult to attain. It came only after sincere searching, prayer, reading the scriptures, and attempting to live a life of pure virtue and love. Then suddenly one day, after a month of such effort, a presence literally descended upon me, surrounded and enveloped me. I was instantly filled with a joy beyond comprehension, a peace beyond under-standing, and an unconditional love for all mankind. This kind of joy, peace, and love is something one never experiences in normal everyday life. I knew I had encountered God.

I have only had this experience once in my life. I could never keep it because in ordinary, everyday life, I could not experience love for all mankind. There were people I disliked, people who were simply an irritation, and people for which I had nothing in common. I had my own life to live. I could never be completely devoted out of love for the good of all mankind. God is love, but I am not. I could not sacrifice my life totally for others because it did not make me happy, and without happiness, one does not have the fuel to go on living.

During the twenty-eight years I lived in California, I returned to Salt Lake City only twice. The first time was when Ruth had turned eighteen. I called her on the phone and asked her if she would go out with me, but she refused. She was going steady with a boy she had known for three years in high school, and whom she later married. Her mother gave me a beautiful photograph which had been taken of her. Her hair still had the color of pure, radiant gold. I kept the picture for several days, but returned it to them before I left to go back to California. Ruth's younger sister had answered the door, and I gave it to her, trying to hold back the tears in my eyes. I did not feel I had the right to keep it.

The next time I returned to Utah, Frank had died and his wife and her brother Nephi were living in the house which was now hers. Frank had left a number of apartments to his wife which provided a steady income. In addition, he had left a house to each of his children. Not bad for a man who had only one arm. Frank had done well.

I asked if I could see a picture of Ruth, and was surprised when her mother gave me the same picture I had been given before of Ruth as a young girl. However, when I looked at it, Ruth somehow looked different. There seemed to be a small imperfection in her face which detracted from her beauty. Why had I not noticed it before? I knew that this was the same exact picture I had seen years earlier, yet somehow it was different. Ruth's face seemed to switch back and forth between the girl I had known and her image in the picture, as if it was some sort of trick photograph.

Had I been bewitched? Had God cast a spell on me, so that the woman I loved was the most beautiful woman in the world to me, while only others could see her as she really was? Or was it that only I could see her true beauty and everyone else saw only an illusion? It did not matter. It did not change my feelings for her.

When I drove out to Ruth's place, she invited me in and asked me—twice—if I wanted a beer. She had thought I had not heard her the first time. I knew it was her way of telling me she was no longer a faithful Mormon, as drinking was against the Mormon religion. She had also acquired the habit of smoking. I did not tell her that I was no longer a Mormon myself.

Ruth's children, a boy and a girl, had grown up and left home. I liked her husband. In many ways, he seemed like a better man than myself. I was happy for Ruth. He had given her a good life, something I could not have done. We visited for a few minutes, and then I left.

As I drove away, Ruth waved from the front yard. She had gone outside to water the lawn, perhaps because she did not want her husband to see her bid me farewell. It would be the last time I would ever see her, but she would always be in my heart.

# Chapter 12

I am now eighty-two years old. Pam is still the only girl I have ever kissed. I did not know that the first time I made love would be my last. Perhaps this was my own choice, perhaps destiny, or perhaps because of what I am. For psychologically, I am still twenty-six years old. My life has remained as if frozen in time, and for me, the events related here happened as if it were yesterday.

My most precious memory of Ruth is walking over to her home one evening to pay the rent. It was dark outside, and I was astonished when she opened the door wearing only her bathrobe. She told me that her parents were not home, but invited me in anyway. As I took a seat on the couch, she sat in a chair opposite me writing a receipt for the rent. I sat transfixed, gazing at her in wonder as the light from the lamp filtered through the strands of her golden hair, illuminating her face in a serene radiance. The soft texture of her light-blue bathrobe outlined the perfect form of her body and caressed her skin in a warm, intimate embrace. It was as if I was looking at the young Virgin Mary. When I left her house, the tears streamed down my face. I knew I would never be worthy of her.

My parents had moved back to Salt Lake City and my sister was taking care of them in their old age. I also moved back shortly after the 9/11 Twin Tower disaster, as I could no longer find work in California in the electronics industry and my sister needed some help.

My mother passed away at the age of ninety-two. In her old age she had been confined to a wheelchair, and I often wheeled her around the neighborhood so that she could get out of the house and enjoy some sunshine, fresh air, and a change of scenery. Whatever problems we had had in the past now seemed irrelevant.

After she was gone, I suddenly came to the realization one day that she had had all the symptoms of having been sexually abused as a child. A relative confirmed that an uncle had been responsible, and when I confronted my father with the matter, he simply remained silent. My father died several years later at the age of ninety-five.

It is a tragedy that the lessons we learn in life come with a price—that the past cannot be changed and we must live with the pain of what could have been.

While in California, I had gone to a Vietnamese place to get a haircut. The young Vietnamese girl who cut my hair not only did an excellent job, but she was also beautiful. When I arrived, there were usually other guys waiting in line for her. However, I felt sorry for her companion who also cut hair, but not nearly as well. She was plain and unattractive and had few customers. Her name was Tu.

One day as I was waiting for a haircut, Tu got up and began combing her long hair in the mirror. She caught me watching her and seemed to enjoy the attention. As I watched in fascination, it was suddenly as if we were alone in the room and she was grooming herself just for me. When she glanced at me, an inner beauty seemed to emerge. She had a certain look which made her stunningly beautiful. I was entranced. I suddenly realized that whereas the other girl wore her beauty on the outside, Tu kept hers hidden on the inside.

Tu had always seemed unaffected and unhurt by the attention paid the other girl, as if she knew her own worth and was waiting only for someone to discover it. I walked up to her and asked if she would cut my hair. She smiled knowingly.

When she had finished, she handed me a mirror to see if I was satisfied. I checked my haircut, then caught her reflection in the mirror and said, "You look just fine." Thinking she had misunderstood me, she said nothing. However, the next time she cut my hair and handed me the mirror, I caught her reflection in the mirror and said again, "You look just fine." This time she laughed.

I went there one last time. I did not want to spoil by repeated visits the intimacy and enchantment of the moment we had shared between us. And besides, I was old enough to be her grandfather.

Throughout life I have had other such treasured moments, which I keep filed away in a special place within my memory. Sometimes in a quiet moment, when I am in a melancholy mood, I take them out and look at them. They have made my life worth living.

I will never forget Pam's parting words. I have often wondered what she meant when she said, "Someday we'll meet again."

# Afterword

In 1977, a book about a haunted house called *The Amityville Horror* was published and became a best seller. It was later made into a movie. Since the author alleged it was a true story, I purchased the book and read it with fascination. Could this really be true, I wondered. The incidents in the book seemed almost beyond belief.

Years later I happened to be listening to a radio talk show which featured the author speaking about his book. The author confessed the book was not true and that you would have to be very naïve to believe it. He had originally asserted the story was true only so the book would sell more copies and would be more exciting to read. All this was done in fun, of course, a sort of practical joke on the reader.

As a youth, I had been entranced by stories of flying saucers and had avidly read two books by George Adamski called *Flying Saucers Have Landed* and *Flying Saucers From Outer Space* in which he claimed that he had been visited by beings from other worlds and that the planets Venus, Mars, Jupiter, Saturn and even the moon were all inhabited by superior beings. These beings had contacted Adamski to show us on earth that we were not alone in the universe and that it was possible to live in peace and harmony without conflict and war.

Adamski's stories were so believable and wonderful. He seemed so honest and sincere. On some days, I believed in flying saucers and on other days, when I was more rational, I did not. Of course, now we know there was no truth to his stories. We have been to the moon and sent probes to the planets and found that none are inhabited.

In a way, believing such stories were true, or that they even might be true, enhanced my enjoyment of reading them. However, such allegations of truth—or in actuality untruth—do a great disservice to the reader, to science in general, and to our search for truth. For if some people lie, while others tell the truth, then how are we to tell the difference? How are we to discover what is true and what is false?

Unfortunately, there is no way to tell. However, I still like to keep an open mind. More recently, I have enjoyed reading about near-death experiences. Some of these may have really happened, and others perhaps not. However, I don't believe that it would be beneficial to ignore all such paranormal occurrences. Life is too complex and its mysteries too deep that we should simply accept what we normally experience and reject everything else.

The reader should not suppose that I am immersed in such reading. Such books have been incidental to my life. I think of myself as a rational person. However, I am always willing to consider viewpoints and experiences opposite to my own.

The supernatural events I have related here are true. They actually happened. I am not trying to fool you or play a practical joke.

Actually, encounters with the supernatural are not rare, but common. Many people have had them. Usually they do not talk about them because such incidents are of a personal nature or they fear they may be subject to ridicule or derision. However, if you have had such an experience yourself, you will often find people will tell you about their encounters with the supernatural once you have shared one of your own.

If you think that the story I have told is painful for me to tell, you would be right. However, it is also a story that fills me with a quiet happiness. For my life was what it was meant to be. It was Ruth's destiny to get married and raise a family, something for which I was never prepared. And I know I could never have made Pam happy. She was meant to have fun in life, and I had a lot of lessons to learn. So while these memories fill me with pain, they also make me grateful to have experienced a love for two beautiful women—an angel of light and an angel of night.

The enchanting beauty of the feminine nature is something that fills me with wonder. It seems there are an infinite number of ways it is revealed, and each one unveils an aspect of the divine.